THE 21ST CENTURY

CANNABIS

FARMING

Growing Green: A Complete Manual for Newcomers to Modern Marijuana Cultivation

Written and Edited by

GABRIEL VONNEGUT

Table of Contents

INTRODUCTION

Welcome to "The 21st Century Cannabis Farming," a thorough book that will take you on a tour through today's dynamic and ever-changing scene of cannabis growing. In these pages, we'll look at the cutting-edge methods, technologies, and sustainable practices that shape the cannabis business today.

Whether you're a seasoned farmer wanting to remain ahead of the competition or a beginner ready to get into the fascinating world of cannabis cultivation, this book is your go-to reference. Prepare to dig into the most recent discoveries, best practices, and technologies influencing the production of one of the most fascinating plants of our time.

From comprehending the science of production to navigating legal and environmental issues, "The 21st Century Cannabis Farming" is your guide to realizing the full potential of cannabis cultivation in the twenty-first century.

Cannabis has long been a maligned plant. Cannabis stigma began in the 1930s and persists to this day in many places. Consider reading about Harry Anslinger's blatantly racist campaign to discredit cannabis. Others, more thinking people, believe cannabis was important in helping early humans to transition from hunting and gathering culture to settle along fertile river bottoms and begin agricultural and livestock cultivation. Regardless, cannabis should not be stigmatized; it has several useful applications.

Much like cauliflower, broccoli, and Brussels sprouts were all produced from the same plant, Brassica oleracea, Cannabis sativa has been cultivated to produce fiber, food, and medications through plant breeding. Cannabis can be planted tightly for fiber and grain production, or with broader (5-by-5-foot) spacing for flower production, in which case a cannabis field can resemble a Christmas tree operation.

Cannabis plants come in both male and female varieties. Males are needed to pollinate female plants in order to produce fiber and grain. Male plants have little utility after that, and they wither and die away. (This might be extended to the utility of human men, but I'd prefer not.)

Before you start stretching your green thumb, be sure it's legal in your state to grow marijuana at home for personal use. While marijuana possession is prohibited at the federal level in the United States, several states allow you to grow your own. The disadvantage is that each has distinct limits on the number of plants you may grow.

It's critical to keep up with the ever-changing rules in your jurisdiction.

Marijuana plants' anatomy may differ based on their sex. Cannabis plants, like humans, are normally either male or female. They can, however, be hermaphrodites. This implies that they have both male and female reproductive organs. These details are critical to understand since detecting sex early can save an entire crop from being pollinated. Knowing which portions of the plant to train can also result in larger, frostier buds on any female plant. When cloning, it's also vital to understand marijuana plant structure so that a cutting may be obtained without killing the plant.

ANATOMY OF THE MARIJUANA PLANT

> **ROOTS:** As previously stated, there are numerous elements of the marijuana plant that are shared by both male and female plants. One of them is roots. These are essentially the marijuana plant's lifeline. When the roots are unhealthy, the whole plant suffers. Roots transport nutrients and water from the growing medium to all parts of the plant. Cannabis roots are fibrous and lengthy. The tap root is the major root, and secondary roots sprout all around it.

> **STEMS:** The main stem develops from the major root, followed by stalks and leaves. As part of the transportation system, the stem collaborates with the roots. Furthermore, the stem serves as the primary support for the entire plant. This allows other stalks and leaves to grow up and out, so the plant can reach its full growth potential

- **INTER-NODES AND NODES:** Nodes run along the stem and are an important aspect of marijuana plant structure. Nodes are the locations on the stem from which further branches will sprout. These are necessary not just for growing larger plants, but also for individuals who want to clone or train their plants. Cutting and training are frequently performed quite near to the node. As a result, anyone interested in growing marijuana must be aware of the location of these nodes. The gaps between these nodes have their own name and are referred to as inter-nodes.

- **STIPULES:** A stipule may be created when a new node is established. These stipules commonly take the appearance of thorns in other plants, such as roses. These shield the plant from things like pests. They resemble a little dagger in the marijuana plant, but they are harmless. In fact, the stipule is one part of the plant in which no one really knows its purpose.

- **FAN LEAVES:** Every marijuana plant, male or female, will have leaves. The leaves are the foundation of any weed plant. Marijuana plant development is heavily reliant on the leaves. Weed leaves absorb all of the light that the plant receives, as well as part of the moisture in the air. They also transfer all of those nutrients to the rest of the plant via photosynthesis. Weed leaves can be defoliated as well.

This implies that the leaves can be removed at various stages of development. When there are a lot of fan leaves, this is done. By removing some of them, light and air may travel more freely about the plant. This can lead to increased yields as well as a healthier plant. As well as lowering the likelihood of bud rot and mildew. Stomata are found on the top and bottom of each leaf. This literally translates to "mouth" in Greek. These stomata open and close in response to environmental factors. To protect the plant from being waterlogged, the stomata may close. When the plant is dry, it may fully open the stomata to absorb as much water as possible. The look of cannabis leaves may tell us a lot about the plant, from what sort of cannabis variety it is to its overall health. Sativa leaves are generally longer and thinner than indica leaves, which are often thicker and larger.

MARIJUANA PLANTS (FEMALE AND MALE)

The majority of the components of female and male marijuana plants are the same. The reproductive portions, on the other hand, are extremely different. And females have far more of them than males.

> **CALYX AND BRACT:** The bract houses the female reproductive organs. They are green, teardrop-shaped, and thickly coated with resin glands. The calyx is hidden inside the bract and is not visible to the human eye. This is a thin coating that covers the ovule at the flower's base.

> **PISTIL AND STIGMA:** The stigma and pistil are two crucial elements of the female marijuana plant structure. The pistil is the female reproductive organ that is coated with stigmas. These stigmas resemble little hairs. The female plant wants to be fertilized by a male plant by releasing these pistils. It will generate seeds at that time.

Many farmers, however, aim to prevent this. There will be no buds if the female plant is fertilized by the male plant, hence it is critical to learn how to sex cannabis plants early on. That will only occur if the female does not been fertilized and instead focuses on developing flowers or buds.

> **COLAS:** As the buds mature, they will be firmly packed together in a bundle. These bundles are referred to as colas. While there may be several around the plant, the primary cola is located at the very top.

> **TRICHOMES:** Many buds will be coated in trichomes within that cola. These are contained in the plant's DNA to defend it against pests. However, they are most known nowadays for having a high concentration of cannabinoids. THC, in particular, enhances the effects of the plant when eaten.

> **POLLEN BAG:** Pollen sacks are exclusively present on male marijuana plants and are essential for breeding. They have anthers instead, which are pollen sacs attached to the stem by a filament. These reproductive components are collectively referred to as the stamen.

A male plant's pollen sacs are tiny, measuring around five millimeters in length. They resemble a little ball or egg. When the male plant matures, these sacs burst open, releasing pollen into the air and pollinating any surrounding female plants. This is beneficial for breeders who are producing seeds from two vigorous parent plants. However, it is not ideal for growers that want to create beautiful buds. When marijuana plants reach the blooming stage, growers can sex them and eliminate male plants from the growing area.

Many beginning producers prefer to plant marijuana indoors for a variety of reasons, including convenience and confidentiality. However, both indoor and outdoor growth settings have both benefits and drawbacks.

What You Should Know About Outdoor Growing

When humans first encountered cannabis, they encountered outdoor growing landraces that had been living in the wild for some years. We don't know who thought of smoking it, but the key is that they were growing outside.

That suggests outdoor growing operations are effective. All you need to do is discover the perfect climate. It should not be too humid, too dry, too chilly, or too hot. It's not a simple task, but even if you don't have the optimum temperature, altering watering quantities can assist.

Outdoor gardening is far less expensive, thanks to the sun doing the hard work for you. This means no upfront costs for lighting accessories or a higher energy bill. Outdoor gardening, on the other hand, is less dependable, less private, and poses more risk to your plants.

Best Outdoor Growing Strains

Some of the greatest cannabis strains for outdoor production include:

- Early Skunk / Early Queen Feminized
- Gorilla Glue #4 Autoflower
- Kyle's Skywalker OG
- Skywalker Haze by Dutch Passion
- Nikki and Swami's Lemon OG Feminized
- Steve's Dream Queen Feminized
- CBD Mango Feminized

What You Should Know About Indoor Growing

Indoor gardening is a surprisingly inexpensive choice. Sure, you'll need to make an initial investment, but it's not as costly as you would think. Especially if you're planning a tiny grow operation with only a few plants. You might even be able to be inventive and design your own development system. Just make sure there's adequate room for air and that there's no excessive humidity or warmth.

Indoor grow operations allow you to more easily regulate your 'ingredient' quantities or access to other factors that your plants receive. This is something you will not be able to do with outdoor harvests.

While indoor plants produce buds more consistently, they are also more dependable. As a result, they will require more of your time than an outdoor-grown flower.

Here are the average temperatures:

- Young plants: 20-30 Celsius.
- Flowering Stage: 18/26 Celsius.

Different accessories, including as fans and exhaust systems, may be required in enclosed environments.

Best Indoor Growing Strains

Here are some of the finest cannabis strains for beginners interested in indoor growing:

- Northern Lights (NL)
- Skunk #1
- Blue Dream
- Cheese/Blue Cheese
- Blueberry
- OG Kush

In addition to these hybrid strains, autoflowering strains and ruderalis strains are recommended for inexperienced indoor growers.

Cannabinoids and terpenes are organic compounds that both exist in the cannabis plant. However, they vary in many ways, the most noticeable being that terpenes have strong scents whereas cannabinoids do not. Terpenes are abundant in practically all plants, but cannabinoids are found mostly in cannabis plants (though black pepper, echinacea, and some other plants contain cannabinoids). In terms of legality, cannabinoids in concentrations of 0.3% or above are prohibited. Many terpenes are lawful and are found in everyday items such as fragrances and cleaning goods.

Terpenes have no effect on the endocannabinoid system, whereas cannabinoids do. Terpenes can contribute to the entourage effect since they do affect various receptor systems in the body. Terpenes may influence how cannabinoids behave in the body even if they do not directly affect the ECS. This means that the terpene composition of a cannabis variety is critical in defining the effect of a certain cultivar (chemotype) of cannabis.

It should also be noted that cannabinoids and terpenes are both officially members of a wide family of chemical compounds known as "terpenoids." Cannabinoids (phytocannabinoids) in cannabis are produced from a diterpene structure. This means that the two types of compounds are more similar than we may expect. Terpenes may also have a "cannabimimetic" effect, meaning that they can imitate the behavior and feelings of cannabinoids without necessarily activating the ECS.

Cannabinoids are chemical compounds that have the ability to modulate the endocannabinoid system. They are classed as phytocannabinoids, meaning they are generated by plants like cannabis, or endocannabinoids, which are produced by the human body. According to research, there are around 150 distinct cannabinoids. Cannabimimetics are man-made synthetic cannabinoids and compounds that imitate the various effects of cannabis.

Cannabinoids: How Do They Work?

Cannabinoids work by binding to cannabinoid receptors. When a cannabinoid attaches to a receptor, a chain reaction occurs that produces a variety of physiological and psychological effects. These receptors, which are found throughout the human body and brain, are classified as CB1 and CB2.

Here are some examples of common cannabinoids:

+ **Tetrahydrocannabinol:** Tetrahydrocannabinol (THC) is the most well-known cannabinoid and is responsible for the psychoactive effects of cannabis products. While many individuals like this cannabinoid for the high it produces, it also has a variety of additional applications. THC products have been shown in studies to be effective in cancer therapy, chronic pain reduction, Alzheimer's disease treatment (in conjunction with CBD), and Parkinson's disease symptom reduction. This cannabinoid also increases appetite, which may aid in the treatment of hunger problems.

+ **Cannabidiol:** Cannabidiol (CBD) is frequently referred to as a "medicinal cannabinoid," which means it has medicinal properties. However, this is a deceptive name because THC has medicinal benefits. CBD-infused products have been shown to be useful in encouraging the creation of new brain cells, lowering brain inflammation, and treating neuron damage, among other cognitive advantages. Other therapeutic applications have been identified, such as the treatment of autoimmune encephalitis, multiple sclerosis, anxiety, and chronic pain.

- **Cannabinol:** Cannabinol (CBN) is a THC metabolite that has earned the moniker "sleepy cannabinoid" due to its effectiveness in treating insomnia. According to research, it is beneficial as a peripheral analgesic, a therapy for glaucoma, and a technique to postpone the onset of amyotrophic lateral sclerosis.

- **Cannabigerol:** Cannabigerolic acid (CBGA) is a precursor of THCA and CBDA, which when heated create CBG, THC, and CBD. CBG has several advantages, including appetite stimulation, which can lead a person's food consumption to more than double. This effect may be beneficial in conditions such as wasting syndrome (cachexia). CBG may also be beneficial in lowering neuroinflammation, delaying the progression of cancer, and treating inflammatory bowel disease (IBD).

Terpenes are a class of aromatic hydrocarbon-based compounds generated by numerous plants, most notably the cannabis plant. They are frequently attributed to the flavor and aroma characteristics of cannabis; nevertheless, studies indicate that they can also have considerable medicinal effects. There are over 30,000 terpenes found in plant species, 220 of which exist in cannabis.

Terpenes: How Do They Work?

Terpenes work by binding to numerous receptors, including GABA receptors, adenosine receptors, and, in the case of beta-caryophyllene, cannabinoid receptors themselves.

The following are some examples of cannabis terpenes:

- **Pinene:** Pinene, as the name suggests, is a terpene having a pine-like fragrance. Pine trees, rosemary, and basil, as well as cannabis, contain it. When used topically, pinene, like other terpenes, has powerful anti-inflammatory effects. When administered topically, it also lowers UV damage to skin and DNA. Individuals who received pinene injections also showed a reduction in the amount of stroke-related brain damage.

- **Myrcene:** Another terpene present in cannabis is myrcene. It exists in many fruits, plants, and essential oils and has an earthy spicy flavor. Myrcene, according to research, produces some of the sedative effects of cannabis. In osteoarthritis, it can also relieve peripheral discomfort and delay cartilage deterioration. It may help minimize cell death in lung cancer patients' lung tissue.

- **Linalool:** Linalool may be found in cannabis and lavender flowers. It is responsible for the anxiety-reducing effects of some cannabis strains and produces a lovely flowery aroma. This terpene, like myrcene, has pain-relieving and calming effects.

- **Limonene:** Limonene is a citrus-scented terpene found in lemon and orange peels. It also exists in cannabis, where it is believed to provide energizing effects. It's been used to treat low energy conditions like chronic fatigue syndrome and depression. It also showed significant tumor shrinkage, particularly in breast cancer.

- **Eucalyptol:** Eucalyptol has a refreshing and minty aroma. This flavor is derived from cannabis, rosemary, wormwood, bay leaves, and its namesake, eucalyptus. Although it may come as no surprise if you've ever used eucalyptus to treat a cold, eucalyptol is effective in the treatment of numerous respiratory illnesses, including asthma, bronchitis, and rhinosinusitis. As part of an essential oil, eucalyptol has also shown anticancer effects and the capacity to enhance cognitive performance in older people.

How Do Cannabinoids and Terpenes Interact?

Terpenes and cannabinoids are not distinct in cannabis. The entourage effect occurs when these two chemical compounds work together. This happens when terpenes and cannabinoids work together to modulate the overall effect of cannabis use. It is widely assumed that the complete spectrum of cannabis-related compounds (terpenes, cannabinoids, and so on) is necessary to create the various effects of cannabis.

Terpenes can alter the amount of THC that penetrates the blood-brain barrier and hence modulate its effects. This connection has the potential to dramatically benefit cannabis users. Knowledgeable persons may forecast the sort of effect cannabis will have with some accuracy by evaluating the types and levels of terpenes and cannabinoids in the product.

Although terpenes may influence how cannabinoids work, and there are many parallels in chemical structure, there is presently no proof that terpenes, with the exception of beta-caryophyllene, act directly on the endocannabinoid system. Terpenes, on the other hand, have a wide range of effects on the body, including serotonin, dopamine, and GABA receptors. This means that various terpenes can contribute to the entourage effect.

You have several options for cannabis grow medium. Here are some of the most prevalent methods of cultivating cannabis, along with the benefits and drawbacks of each.

Soil

When growing cannabis outdoors, you can utilize natural soil and sunshine to perform the majority of the job, and many people prefer the results in terms of fragrance, taste, and effects. Growing outdoors, on the other hand, might be legally problematic, with many more variables to consider.

Indoor grows may also use soil, and many people prefer to use soil because it is a natural supply of nutrients and does not require as many additional nutrients from other sources. Good soil is also widely accessible at many gardening supply stores.

Pros

- Cannabis has better taste, smell, and effects.

Cons

- Concerns about the weather.
- Concerns about the law.
- Pests.
- Thieves.
- Animals in the wild.
- Water and sunshine must be carefully balanced.

- Only two harvests each year are possible (depending on your environment).
- Overall challenging.

Coco Coir

Coco coir is a natural fiber derived from the husk of a coconut. It's a growth medium that mixes earth and hydroponic ingredients. It may be blended with soil or used on its own and is a good growth medium for novices.

Pros

- Water retention is excellent.
- Drainage that is dependable.
- A lot of air.
- Roots spend less time hunting for nourishment since you provide them through nutrient water.
- Coco coir has a pH range of 5.2-6.8 that is good for cannabis cultivation.
- Reduces the likelihood of pests, fungus, and other diseases attacking your plant.
- Environmentally friendly and reusable if properly prepared for your next growing cycle.

Cons

- Coir bales are frequently treated with chemicals to prevent them from being infected with diseases, so study the label or visit the manufacturer's website for information on the coir you're using to verify that the chemicals won't interfere with your plant's growth cycle.
- To increase the plant's calcium, magnesium, and iron levels, you'll need coco coir-specific fertilizers.

- Due to being washed in saltwater, some forms of coco coir may have a high salt content. If this is the case, make sure the coir has been cleaned with fresh water.
- You will have to provide the plant nutrients yourself.

Hydroponics

Hydroponics is a method of growing cannabis that use mineral fertilizer solutions in a water solvent. Essentially, the plant will be placed in a container surrounded by an inert growth medium (e.g., perlite, vermiculite, clay aggregate, gravel, or sand) and a nutrient solution will be pumped through the inert material and into the plant (continuous-flow solution culture). In certain procedures, the plant is retained in a nutrient reservoir (static solution culture).

Pros

- Massive, potent yields.

Cons

- Nutrient needs are precise.
- For optimal development, knowledge of various strains is necessary.
- Aerated water is required.
- Experienced growers are better suited.

Aeroponics

In many aspects, aeroponics is similar to hydroponics, except that the plant roots are kept in an aerated chamber soaked with fine droplets of nutritional solution. A thin mist of atomized nutrients is applied to the roots on a regular basis.

When compared to hydroponic grows, aeroponic grows use fewer nutrients and less water, and unlike hydroponically-grown plants, aeroponic grows may be moved to soil media without frightening the plant.

Pros

- High and efficient yields.

Cons

- High initial investment.
- Constant surveillance is required.
- Too much time and worry.

Aquaponics

Aquaponics is a hybrid of hydroponics and aquaculture, or the cultivation of fish and other aquatic organisms in a tank. Aquaponics is a symbiotic habitat in which aquatic creatures' waste feeds the plants growing on top, while the plants reduce hazardous waste levels from the water.

Aquaponics systems have been around for a long time, although they may not have been refined until lately.

Pros

- Water use is minimal.
- There is no need for plant food.
- There is little to no chemical use.
- Pests and illnesses are less likely to attack.
- Cannabis plants thrive in aquaponic systems.

Cons

- Fewer plants because of the smaller grow space.
- Powerful electrical outputs.
- High level of upkeep.
- As the system becomes more complicated, the number of failure sites increases.
- High prices.

The grower must have the proper cannabis grow equipment in order to grow properly. Purchasing equipment is the first step in establishing your grow, and that first cost might make you sweat!

Investing properly throughout the cannabis grow setup stage will pay you in the long run. Once installed, your grow equipment will pay rewards in the long run, and after two or three harvests, you will wonder why you were concerned about the original investment!

With such a large initial investment, it is tempting to attempt to save money by cutting shortcuts, but it is well worth it to invest in the best equipment available.

Outdoor producers have it easier, thanks to a substantially lower investment in cannabis grow equipment - with a shopping list consisting of only pots, grow media, nutrients/fertilizers, and insect control. The drawback is that the outside grower has little control over their grow environment, whereas the indoor grower has complete control!

In this article, we will go over the key equipment that every indoor grower requires for a great yield, including:

- Tents for growing plants
- Ventilation, fans, filters and CO_2
- Temperature and humidity control
- Water supply systems

- Growing mediums
- Fertilizers and nutrients
- Aids for pest control

1. Grow Tents and Grow Spaces

While indoor grow facilities come in many forms and sizes, the grow tent is the most accessible, practical, and cost-effective piece of cannabis grow equipment. This is due to the fact that it can be purchased to fit practically any place and comes ready to plug in and play. **A grow tent area offers:**

- **Space optimizing:** Grow tents are the home grower's best friend. They are small enough to fit into a corner of an attic, cellar, or even a spare bedroom. There are grow tents that accommodate practically any location, including some with sloped rooves to fit beneath lofts.
- **Self-contained environment:** Zip them up and they resemble a temporary closet. When you unzip them, you'll have a self-contained grow environment with ventilation holes in all the correct locations, support for hanging grow lights, and reflective inside material to guarantee uniform light distribution.
- **Climate and odor regulate:** Because it is a self-contained enclosure, the environment can be readily maintained in order to maintain an optimal climate and control the scent.
- **Stealth potential:** There is a wide range of cannabis grow equipment available, including several tiny tents that can fit under a desk or table top or slip into the bottom of a closet.

Cannabis grow tents will often have the following characteristics as standard. However, when purchasing cannabis grow tent, it is always worth paying a bit more to get a high-quality product.

These aspects of grow tent cultivation should be highlighted:

- **Material:** High-quality grow tents are built of long-lasting materials and reflective textiles, which assist to evenly disperse light throughout the plants. Be wary of low-cost generic tents that are of poor quality and may emit offgassing that is detrimental to plants.
- **Ventilation:** Grow tents include various ventilation apertures that allow fans, filters, and ducts to be installed. Proper ventilation guarantees a constant flow of fresh air, reducing heat buildup and preserving ideal humidity levels.
- **Frame:** A strong grow tent frame supports the weight of lights, fans, and filters while maintaining the tent's shape. Most grow tents can accommodate lights weighing 50-70 kilograms (100-150lbs).
- **Grow tent placement:** A key consideration is locating a grow tent so that there is easy access to electricity, ventilation and water supply. It's also crucial to have some breathing room to enable for good plant care (navigating around seedlings is lot simpler than going in there to maintain fully matured plants - especially those in the rear!).
- **Maintaining the growth environment:** Good management practices need assessing humidity, temperature, and plant location on a regular basis to ensure that light is distributed properly.

2. Ventilation, Fans, Filters and CO_2

Just as people thrive in well-ventilated environments, our green friends need a breath of fresh air to thrive. Before we look at the numerous cannabis grow equipment systems that provide crucial ventilation to the grow room, let's look at why it's required.

Ventilation systems aid in the regulation of temperature, humidity, and air exchange within the growth environment. Ventilation protects grow room cannabis plants from excess moisture, mildew, and pests by supplying a steady flow of fresh air and clearing stagnant air.

Air Filters And Extractor Fans

Extractor fans (sometimes referred to as exhaust fans) are the workhorses of grow room ventilation systems and an essential component of cannabis grow equipment. These strong fans remove stale air from the growth space and allow indoor and outdoor air to circulate.

Consider the size of the grow space, the quantity of plants growing, and the heat created by your lighting system when choosing an extractor fan.

The greatest air filter money can buy is necessary for trapping airborne pollutants like dust and pollen, but probably most significantly for collecting the stench of smelly blossoming buds, which may be so strong that half the street will get a whiff.

Carbon Dioxide (CO²) Producers

Carbon dioxide is essential for photosynthesis, which fuels plant development. CO_2 producers come into play in indoor situations with restricted CO_2 levels and are increasingly regarded an important cannabis grow equipment investment.

These gadgets emit precise quantities of carbon dioxide. However, it is critical to monitor and maintain proper CO_2 levels, since too much might hurt your plants and jeopardize their health.

The significance of proper air circulation in the grow room:

- **Preventing hot spots:** These are locations with higher temperatures that might cause problems, such as localized stress points in the grow room (e.g., certain plants become overheated). Small oscillating fans strategically placed around the grow chamber will generate optimum air circulation.
- **Strengthening plant stems:** Air circulation helps to flex the stem which strengthens the stalks of plants, simulating what occurs in the wild when plants have to adapt to the wind. A stronger framework aids in the support of the weight of the buds.
- **Pest and illness prevention:** Proper air circulation keeps bugs from landing and breeding. It also aids in the prevention of mold and mildew growth caused by stale, damp air.

3. Temperature and Humidity Control Grow Equipment

Before we look at the cannabis grow equipment used to manage temperature and humidity in the grow room, let's have a look at why temperature and humidity are so crucial in the cannabis growing process and the varying requirements at each stage of the cannabis grow.

- **Temperature and humidity ideal for cannabis in the stage of vegetation**
  The grow room temperature should be between 21-29°C (70-85°F) during the vegging stage. This temperature range promotes vigorous vegetative growth, photosynthesis, and nutrient intake. A relative humidity (RH) level of 40-70% is good. This temperature range promotes healthy transpiration, nutrition absorption, and foliar development.

- **Ideal blooming temperature and humidity for cannabis**
  Consistent temperatures are required for optimum growth throughout the budding period, with an ideal range of 18-27°C (65-80°F). During this period, cooler nighttime temperatures can boost resin synthesis and improve terpene profiles. Mold and mildew are reduced when humidity levels are reduced to 40-50% RH.

It is critical to achieve the proper temperature and humidity balance. High humidity mixed with high temperatures can foster the growth of mildew, bugs, and diseases, whereas low humidity can cause excessive transpiration and plant stress.

Grow Equipment That Regulates Temperature and Humidity

Here are a few items of cannabis grow equipment that are crucial for maintaining appropriate temperature and humidity levels:

- **Thermometer and hygrometer:** It is critical to invest in a dependable thermometer and hygrometer to correctly monitor the temperature and humidity in the grow environment.
- **Ventilation and air circulation:** Extractor fans, intake fans, and oscillation fans aid in the removal of stale air, the introduction of fresh air, and the adjustment of temperature and humidity.
- **Dehumidifiers and humidifiers:** Dehumidifiers and humidifiers can be used to modify humidity levels depending on your unique demands. In tropical grow rooms, dehumidifiers are popular for removing excess moisture from the air.
- **Climate management systems:** In larger-scale activities or regions with extreme climates, HVAC systems and climate control equipment offer precise oversight over humidity, temperature, and airflow.

Keep in mind that cannabis plants grow in a consistent and regulated atmosphere. Regular monitoring, temperature and humidity adjustments, and optimum ventilation are required for healthy development and the prevention of concerns such as mold, mildew, and insect infestations.

4. Watering Systems for Cannabis Cultivation Equipment

Aside from hand watering, several irrigation systems can help to enhance efficiency and give regular hydration to your cannabis plants.

Let's look at little common cannabis grow equipment watering system options:

- **Drip irrigation systems:** Use a network of tubes and emitters to provide water directly to the base of each plant, giving accurate and focused watering, reducing water waste, and allowing for effective nutrient absorption. Drip irrigation is great for bigger installations and may be automated for added ease.
- **Wick System:** A wick system may be a very inexpensive and beneficial solution to employ for modest crops.
- **Sprinkler systems:** These are more commonly utilized in outdoor growth, although they may also be modified for inside application. Sprinklers spray or sprinkle water over a greater area, but they must be properly installed to avoid difficulties such as mold caused by overwatering.
- **Hydroponics:** This method of cannabis cultivation employs a nutrient solution based on water that circulates around the plant roots, delivering both water and nutrients.

5. Cannabis growing equipment for various cultivation mediums

While not exactly cannabis grow equipment, selecting the correct medium and container for your pot plants is an important aspect of the process.

Most producers begin using soil, but many will change their medium as their knowledge of cannabis growing techniques expands.

The most often used cannabis growing mediums:

- **Cannabis cultivation in soil:** Soil is a healthy environment for your plants since it is high in organic matter and helpful bacteria. Choose high-quality, well-draining soil mixtures designed exclusively for cannabis growth. Many gardeners build their own soil mix.
- **Cannabis cultivation in coco coir:** Coco coir, which is made from coconut husks, has become popular as a flexible growth media. It is usually combined with other ingredients to make a balanced substrate for cannabis plants.
- **Hydroponic cannabis cultivation:** Hydroponics is a soilless growing technology that feeds the plants with a nutrient-rich water solution. It enables for more accurate nutrition distribution and quicker development rates.

Cannabis cultivation in containers:

- **Garden pots:** Plastic pots are the most commonly used for cannabis cultivation. Choose a size that allows your plants' root systems, permitting room for development while preventing over-crowding. In general, the larger the pot, the larger the plant.

- **Smart Pots:** These permeable containers (also known as textiles pots) increase root health by promoting improved ventilation and preventing root binding. Smart pots come in a variety of sizes, making them appropriate for various stages of plant growth.

6. Cannabis cultivation equipment for pest control

Diligence is the grower's finest tool, and implementing an Integrated Pest Management System (IPM) is strongly encouraged - a mix of preventative measures, excellent practice in the grow room, regular visual checks and targeted treatments.

These cannabis grow equipment recommendations (some of which are living tools) can aid with pest control:

- **Organic sprays:** Such as neem oil, insecticidal soaps, and plant extracts, can be beneficial in pest management.
- **Clean Clothing and gloves:** Getting into the habit of changing clothing (even if it's just new shoes and an overcoat) keeps pests and diseases from entering the grow area. Disposable gloves are an important piece of cannabis equipment while working with diseased plants.
- **Beneficial insects:** These are predatory allies of cannabis growers and natural adversaries of many pests that feed on cannabis plants, such as aphids, spider mites, and thrips. Predators such as ladybugs, lacewings, and predatory mites provide a good natural defense.

If you're growing marijuana indoors, you should understand the significance of grow lights, which offer the essential light energy for photosynthesis and bud formation. With so many options on the market, selecting the best cannabis grow lights may be difficult.

In this post, we'll look at the many types of grow lights available and help you understand their particular benefits and drawbacks. We'll also go over why cannabis grow lights are required, as well as how to fine-tune your lighting to produce a better growing environment.

Three Types of Cannabis Grow Lights

There are three basic types of cannabis grow lights to consider: HID (high-intensity discharge), LED (light-emitting diode), and CFL (compact fluorescent lamp). Each kind has its own set of perks and disadvantages.

1. HID Grow Lamps:

They are recognized for their high intensity and may provide adequate light to cannabis plants for the entirety of their growing cycle. These lights may give strong, penetrating light that helps cannabis plants thrive and contributes to pleasing harvests.

However, HID lights consume more energy than alternative solutions, increasing the expense of your electric bill. Furthermore, they create a lot of heat, which can be dangerous if not adequately regulated. Adequate ventilation and cooling systems are required to maintain appropriate temperatures in the growth space.

2. LED Grow Lights

Because of their energy efficiency and extended lifespan, LED lights have grown in favor among cannabis farmers. Because they use less power than HID lights, they are considered a more cost-effective option in the long term. Furthermore, because they last longer, they require less maintenance and replacement.

Another advantage of LED lights is their light spectrum diversity. They may be programmed to give certain wavelengths of light ideal for different phases of weed plant growth, promoting optimum photosynthesis. They also generate less heat.

The greater initial cost of LED grow lights is a stumbling block for some farmers. Despite the initial outlay, their energy efficiency and longevity make them an excellent choice.

3. CFL Grow Lights

CFL lights are an inexpensive and easily available solution that is especially popular among novices or small-scale producers. They provide less intense light, which is ideal for seedlings, clones, or young plants in their early stages of development.

To give a more broad light spectrum, CFL lights can be used in conjunction with other types of cannabis grow lights. They are quite small and do not produce excessive heat, so you can set them closer to plants without fear of harm.

While CFL lights are inexpensive and convenient, their limitations should not be overlooked. They may not be sufficient for larger, more established plants that demand higher light levels due to their lower intensity. when a result, when cannabis plants mature, farmers frequently switch to more powerful lighting solutions.

The Most Important Advantages of Using Grow Lights for Cannabis Cultivation

Cannabis grow lights are essential in indoor cultivation because they replicate the natural sunlight necessary for photosynthesis. They offer steady light intensity, which enables gardeners to adjust and optimize plant growing conditions.

Here are three significant advantages of adding marijuana grow lights in your grow space:

+ **Controlling the Light Spectrum:** Different phases of cannabis development require different light spectrums, such as blue for vegetative growth and red for blooming. Most grow lights may be adjusted to offer the optimal spectrum for each stage of growth.
+ **Year-Round Cultivation:** With grow lights, growing marijuana can be carried out irrespective of the outdoor weather or seasonal changes. This assures a steady and consistent supply of cannabis plants.

↓ **Increased Yields:** Proper illumination promotes healthy plant growth, bud development, and resin production, which helps optimize yields. High-grade marijuana grow lights help to increase the potency and overall quality of the cannabis produced.

4 Things to Think About Before Making a Purchase

1. Plant Growth Stages and Light Intensity Requirements

First and foremost, evaluate the type/stage of cannabis plants you are growing under that light. Are we talking about veg-stage cannabis grow lights? Or plants in the blooming stage? Perhaps both? Cannabis adores the beauty of a complete spectrum of lights. However, there are some interesting changes in the illumination spectrum required by different phases of development. If you master them, your plants will grow faster!

Your plants require low to medium intensity light with more blue in the spectrum during the veg stage. Why? Plants have an evolutionary tendency to strive toward the sky, which is known as positive phototropism.

When it is time for blossoming, everything changes. Your cannabis plants require bright light and a spectrum that is predominantly red. The red light assists them in the formation of those lovely blossoms while also reminding them, "Hey, stop growing stems and leaves; it's time to get busy with those blooms!"

If you require a cannabis grow light for both stages, you should use a broad spectrum light with adjustable intensity. When it comes to selecting the best grow light for your cannabis, light intensity is crucial.

2. The Size of Your Growing Area

Now, let's look at another essential factor: the size of your growing area. If you're working in a tiny or constrained location, you'll need a marijuana grow lamp that can provide the proper intensity and spectrum without turning your grow room into a sweaty sauna.

For many of these settings, LED fixtures are the obvious solution. This is because they produce high-intensity output while producing little heat. This is especially crucial for micro-growers, who frequently struggle to keep temperatures under control in rooms without A/C, air exchange, and extensive environmental controls.

LED lights provide a narrow beam of light with little dispersion. This may not be a worry for growers with tiny locations, but it is something to consider when constructing larger weed tents. Indeed, because to their low energy consumption, high intensity output, and simplicity of environmental management, LED lights have been adopted by many commercial grow facilities and greenhouses.

3. Energy Conservation

When it comes to energy usage, this is also something to consider. LED lights are the most energy efficient. They have an amazing capacity to turn power into light with little waste. In contrast to double-ended (DE) or classic high-pressure sodium (HPS) lighting, LED lights do not waste energy or emit heat.

Most HPS and DE fixtures consume 1000 watts, but LED lights with comparable or even better PPFD output need 500-600 watts. Growers may now place LED lights considerably closer to the canopy, resulting in improved light usage and more balanced canopy development. However, installing DE-HPS lights less than 2 feet away from the canopy can burn and harm your plants.

LED lights for cannabis cultivation are the most cost-effective choice. Their high efficiency reduces the demand for HVAC systems and substantial environmental interventions. LED lights aid to minimize energy expenses by needing fewer equipment and resources.

4. Consider your budget

A cannabis grow lamp is a long-term investment. While it may be tempting to go with the cheapest choice, investing in a higher-quality one within your budget usually results in a more reliable and lasting lighting solution for your cannabis plants.

CFL lights are the most cost-effective choice, with prices ranging from $10 to $50 per bulb or fixture. HID lights are reasonably priced. They might cost you anything from $50 to $300. LED lights, as previously said, always have a greater starting cost. An entry-level LED built for small-scale systems might cost between $50 and $200. Higher-end LED lights can cost anywhere from $200 to over $1000.

Set up the Proper Lighting to Promote Cannabis Growth

To maintain healthy cannabis development, you need first understand the notion of PPFD (photosynthetic photon flux density). Plant photosynthetic activity is determined by PPFD, which quantifies the intensity of light received by plants. One of the major aspects in determining the ideal PPFD level is the concentration of CO_2 in the grow area.

Another measure to consider is PAR (photosynthetically active radiation), which refers to the spectral range of light that plants may employ for photosynthesis. PAR and PPFD are ideas that are closely connected. PPFD may be thought of as a measure of the amount of PAR that reaches a certain surface area per unit of time.

Each stage of cannabis growth needs a different level of PPFD and PAR. Seedlings and clones, for example, require lower PPFD values (about 200-400 mol/m2/s), whereas vegetative and blooming phases require higher values (approximately 600-1000 mol/m2/s). Growers may calculate how many cannabis grow lights they need for optimal coverage and intensity, as well as how far they should be from the plants, by calculating lighting demands based on the size of the growing space and desired PPFD values.

It's also worth noting that managing the concentration of CO_2 in the grow room is essential for getting the finest outcomes. Variations in CO_2 concentration have been found in studies to have a considerable impact on the photosynthetic response, growth, and water usage efficiency of cannabis sativa. Plant productivity and production can be improved by maintaining an adequate CO_2 level, often between 1000-1500 ppm (parts per million).

There are various factors to consider while selecting the ideal seeds for your success. It all boils down to what you require, desire, and already have (space, energy, and so on).

Where and how will you grow?

There are a few quick ways to narrow down your selections before selecting your seeds. First, decide where and how you will grow your cannabis. So, do you cultivate indoors or outdoors? If so, how is the weather? Which would you rather have, hydro or soil? Do you have any experience growing or training cannabis plants?

Using the information in all of these questions, you can determine the best strain for your company. Naturally, whether you're growing indoors or outdoors, the quantity of area available will influence the specimen you select.

Examine the Seed Descriptions!

Always inspect the cannabis seeds for important information to ensure that you know precisely what you're getting. This allows you to identify a strain's potential effects and flavor, as well as its ease of growing, prospective yields, and harvest time.

Things to Consider When Choosing Cannabis Seeds

- Sativa, Indica, Hybrid
- Medical or Recreational Cannabis
- Feminized, Auto-Flowering, Regular Photoperiod
- Climate
- Easy and Advanced
- Price.

Marijuana Seed Types (Feminized, Regular, and Auto-Flowering)

- **Auto-flowering seeds:** Auto-flowering seeds create plants that bloom without the requirement for a shift in the light cycle. This seed type is recommended for new gardeners due to its rapid growth and low care needs. Auto-flowering has excellent genetics and is also noted for its durability. As a result, while growing in your garden, they will be able to endure mold and bug infestations. Plant owners benefit from reduced daylight needs since it makes scheduling easier.

- **Feminized Cannabis Seeds:** Feminized cannabis seeds only yield female cannabis plants that blossom. As previously said, these female plants are ideal for growers seeking highly concentrated cannabis. Instead of reproducing, unfertilized females will spend their energy to produce Sensimilla, a powerful cannabinoid. These sticky buds are powerful cannabis forms that are commonly available in supermarkets.

- **Regular Seeds:** A man and a female create regular seeds together. You won't know the gender of your plant until it begins to blossom. If you want to grow high-quality buds that contain cannabinoids, you must separate the male and female seeds.

Gender segregation impedes seed production and pollination, which spreads spectacularly from 3 to 3.75 kilometers. Male plants are frequently destroyed because to their incapacity to produce cannabinoid-producing flowers. Consumers find the lack of cannabinoids in the finished product unattractive. They generate both genders and are genetically unchanged, allowing for the creation of new seeds.

Best Marijuana Seeds

- **Girl Scout Cookies** - Best marijuana seeds overall
- **Widow** -excellent for growing outdoors.
- **Jack Herer Fast** - Blooms in 6-7 weeks
- **Super Silver Haze** - Potent Sativa seeds
- **Lambs Breath** - Bob Marley's "favorite" strain
- **Skywalker OG** - High 23% THC content
- **Banana Kush** - Great Kush seeds
- **Durban Poison** - Fantastic regular breeding seeds
- **Super Skunk** - Excellent for beginners.
- **Critical Mass** - 5% CBD is suitable for medical use.

Factors That Determines Marijuana Seed Pricing

Understanding the elements that determine cannabis seed pricing will assist you in finding the greatest deal when purchasing cannabis seeds.

- **Genetics**
  Quality genetics can command a higher price than other varieties. Nonetheless, if you purchase from a reputed seed bank or breeder, you may obtain high-quality seeds at a reasonable price. Because the breeder has toiled for years to establish a stable, tasty, and fragrant strain, high-quality seeds are more costly.

- **The Supply and Demand**
  Cannabis seed costs are also affected by supply and demand. If a specific strain is in high demand or has a limited supply, prices may skyrocket. Similarly, cannabis market movements might have an impact on which seeds fetch a premium.

- **The Cannabinoids concentration**
  Higher THC content seedlings often cost more than lower THC concentration seeds. Cannabidiol (CBD) is another prominent cannabinoid that impacts seed costs. CBD with a high concentration costs more than CBD with a low concentration.

- **The Production Costs**
  The cost of each seed is determined by the amount of money, time, and work spent on it. Regular seeds, for example, are less expensive since they do not

demand considerable breeding as is needed to generate a stable feminized, or auto-flowering seed. These seed kinds are more pricey.

Germination is the process by which a seed sprouts and begins to grow. It's an important component of producing cannabis since properly germinating your seeds establishes the basis for how well your plants develop and generate buds.

Cannabis seed germination ensures that they grow into healthy, mature plants with all of the delectable scents and spectacular harvests you desire. You can regulate the quality of your harvest by germinating cannabis seeds. Knowing how to germinate cannabis seeds correctly guarantees that you have enough viable plants to put in their ultimate position when harvest time arrives.

Cannabis Seeds Explained

Cannabis seeds come in a variety of forms and sizes. Some are spherical, others oval, while yet others are long and thin. However, all cannabis seeds contain the same components:

- A coat or outer shell
- A kind of endosperm
- Two cotyledons (embryonic leaves)
- The embryo on its own

When looking for cannabis seeds to germinate, opt for ones that are dark brown or gray in color, since they are of greater quality than lighter-colored ones. The size of your seed is also important; larger seeds have a better probability of germination than smaller ones.

There are many different varieties of cannabis seeds on the market to choose from. **These are some examples:**

- Regular cannabis seeds produce both male and female plants.
- Feminized cannabis seeds are 100% female and generate higher yields than ordinary cannabis seeds.
- After a few weeks, autoflowering seeds begin their flowering cycle on their own.

Choosing high-quality cannabis seeds is critical for effective germination and robust plants with full taste and potency. Look for reliable seed banks that guarantee their products and choose genetically sound seeds.

Preparations for Germination

Proper pre-germination treatments are the best approach to germinate cannabis seeds. You must have the required tools at your disposal, such as

- A thermometer
- pH meter
- A growing medium
- A container in which to germinate your seeds

You should also make sure that your atmosphere is conducive to cannabis seed germination; too much light might hinder sprouting, while too little can result in delayed germination.

It is also critical to properly preserve your cannabis seeds before attempting to develop them. Keep them in an airtight container in a cold, dry environment, ideally between 5°C and 15°C (41°F and 59°F).

Various Cannabis Seed Germination Methods

If you're wondering how to germinate a cannabis seed, there are various options open to you. Here are some of the most often used techniques:

The Paper Towel Technique

This is one of the easiest methods for germinating cannabis seeds and is generally recommended by novices. Simply soak two paper towels in water, rinse them out until moist but not dripping wet, then insert your cannabis seeds between them in a shallow container.

Wrap the top in plastic wrap and place it on a water heater to stay warm. Every few hours, check on the paper towels and replace any that have dried out. It's time to place your cannabis seeds in their final growth media when you notice a little white root emerge from the seed.

Soil Methods

Another popular technique for growing cannabis seeds is the soil approach, sometimes known as "direct sowing." This involves immediately putting your seeds into their final growth medium and exposing them to light. To do this correctly:

- To defend against hot and cold periods; use a quality organic potting mix with sufficient drainage, aeration, and some mulch.
- Plant your cannabis seeds in the dirt approximately 1/4 inch deep and keep them damp (but not wet) until they sprout.
- Make sure the earth is warm but not hot – roughly 21°C (70°F) is good.

The Rockwool Technique

If you're growing marijuana inside, the rockwool approach could be a better choice. Place your cannabis seeds in little holes of rockwool cubes and soak them in water until they're damp but not soggy. Set the cubes on a heating pad set to 21°C (70°F). When your cannabis seeds begin to sprout, place the cubes near a light source and raise the temperature if necessary.

How to Troubleshoot Germination Problems

Cannabis seeds that do not germinate or germinate slowly can be unpleasant for gardeners. Fortunately, you have various options for troubleshooting and resolving these situations.

If your cannabis seeds take too long to sprout, it might be due to a lack of temperature or moisture. As a result, keep the growth medium moist but not wet and at an ideal temperature of approximately 21°C (70°F). If it's still not working, try raising the temperature slightly or looking at other aspects, such as how much light your cannabis seeds are getting.

It's also possible that your cannabis seeds went bad owing to poor storage conditions. This is why it's critical to get cannabis seeds from reliable seed banks and keep them properly stored. Examine your cannabis seeds for evidence of mildew, discolouration, or any other apparent damage that might indicate that they are no longer viable. If this is the case, it is advisable to start from scratch.

Post-germination Care

Once your cannabis seeds have germinated, it is critical to provide them with the proper atmosphere to grow into healthy plants. To get started, gently put your seeds into their growing pots.

Make sure each pot has a drainage hole on the bottom and is filled with excellent soil or another medium rich in nutrients and moisture, such as coco coir. Place your seedlings gently into the earth, taking care not to damage the root system too much.

The key to proper post-germination care is to provide enough light, humidity, and nutrients to your cannabis seedlings. Make sure they get at least 12 hours of strong indirect sunshine every day, as well as adequate ventilation.

Aim for humidity level of 50-60%, and water your cannabis seedlings only when the soil becomes dry, which should be around 2-3 times each week. It is not required to fertilize your cannabis plants at this time, but if you want, use a diluted fertilizer solution with a low nitrogen concentration.

What Is Cannabis Transplanting?

The procedure of shifting a cannabis plant from one growth medium to another is known as transplanting. This may entail moving your plants from a smaller container, such as a single cup, to a larger pot or even right outside into their final growth medium.

When transplanting your plants, it's critical to consider numerous aspects, like the size and height of the new pot, your fertilizer levels or soil pH, and the amount of light they're getting.

Before transplanting your plants, wait until they have formed strong root systems and many nodes. Plants are ready to be transplanted when they have 5-7 nodes (where leaves and branches emerge from the stem).

Why Is Marijuana Plant Transplanting Important?

Transplanting offers various advantages that can dramatically boost yields. Moving plants to a larger container encourages the development of a more strong root system, which results in improved nutrient uptake. Furthermore, this technique allows the plant to have access to more soil, which implies more room for roots to develop, resulting in a much healthier and more prolific cannabis harvest.

It's also worth noting that transplanting your cannabis plants will help them establish stronger structure and grow larger overall. This is especially useful if you want to get the most out of your plants' production.

When Should Marijuana Plants Be Transplanted?

When your cannabis plants have formed a strong root system and multiple nodes, it is time to transplant. This usually occurs at the 5-7 node stage, however it might vary according on the strain. It is critical to handle your cannabis plants with care while transplanting them since their roots are sensitive and easily injured.

When transplanting your plants, you need also consider the surroundings. Avoid transplanting them during hot or cold weather, for example, as this might be stressful for your plants. However, make certain that you have the proper lighting and nutrition levels for the strain you're cultivating.

Cannabis Transplanting Frequently Asked Questions

When is it OK to transfer a solo cup?

When your plant gets 5-7 nodes, you may transplant a single cup. This is the point at which your plants are mature enough to withstand the transplant without becoming unduly stressed.

When is the ideal season to cultivate marijuana?

When your plants have formed a strong root system and multiple nodes, it is time to transplant. According to master growers, this is normally doable at the 5-7 node stage.

When transferring my plants, what environment should I avoid?

Avoid transplanting your plants in extreme heat or cold, since this can be stressful for them. Also, ensure that you have the proper lighting and nutrition levels for the strain you're cultivating.

After two weeks, how large should my plants be?

It varies on the strain, but your plants should be 4-10 inches tall after 2 weeks. They should also have created a strong root system and a number of nodes. They may be ready to be transferred at this stage.

Cannabis cultivation can be an artistic process. There are so many ways to grow the plant and so many different pruning techniques that can bring huge benefits when properly executed. In terms of allowing me to construct the precise form for function to generate the greatest bloom, I see the cannabis plant as a bonsai tree. Pruning and training procedures are critical for maximizing production.

Why Prune and Train Cannabis Outdoors?

Pruning and training are used for a variety of objectives in outdoor cannabis farming. Growers can use these approaches to:

- **Increase Light Penetration:** By cutting extra foliage and establishing an open canopy, more light may reach the plant's lower sections, encouraging bud development and total production.

- **Improve Airflow:** Proper pruning and training procedures allow for more space between branches, which allows for improved airflow. Improved ventilation aids in the reduction of humidity and the prevention of mold and mildew growth.

- **Manage Plant Size:** Growers may manage the size and form of their cannabis plants by pruning and training. This is especially beneficial for preserving discrete gardens and regulating plant height in height-restricted areas

- **Stimulate Bud Development:** Growers can stimulate bigger, denser buds by pruning lower, shaded foliage and concentrate development energy on the major colas.

Pruning Techniques

- **Selective Leaf Removal:** Remove bigger fan leaves that are obscuring bud sites or obstructing light penetration. However, avoid removing too many leaves at once because they are essential for photosynthesis.

- **Topping:** Topping is the process of eliminating the terminal growth of the main shoot in order to promote the formation of many colas. This method promotes bushier growth and increases the number of possible bud sites.

- **Lollipopping:** Lollipopping is the process of reducing lower branches and leaves to concentrate growing energy on the higher canopy. This method increases ventilation and sends nutrients to the highest buds.

- **Defoliation:** During the flowering stage, part of the bigger leaves are removed to expose bud locations and promote light penetration. However, use caution and avoid over-defoliation, which can stress the plant.

Training Techniques

- **LST (Low-Stress Training):** LST is the practice of gently bending and tying down branches to promote horizontal development. This method encourages a more equal canopy and exposes more bud sites to light.

- **SCROG (Screen of Green):** SCROG includes creating a horizontal canopy with a screen or net. Branches are taught to grow through the screen as the plant matures, resulting in an equal canopy with many blossom locations.
- **Supercropping:** Supercropping is the practice of purposefully injuring the plant's stems in order to encourage lateral growth and boost bud output. To avoid injuring the plant, this procedure should be used with caution.

- **Trellising:** Trellising is the process of supporting a plant with pegs, cages, or trellises. This approach aids in the preservation of the plant's structure and protects branches from breaking under the weight of heavy buds.

When Should You Prune and Train?

During the vegetative stage of cannabis growth, pruning and training should be performed. Begin trimming and training early in the season to give the plant time to recuperate and adapt before blossoming. Avoid excessive trimming or training during the flowering period to avoid disrupting bud formation and stressing the plant.

Outdoor cannabis farmers that want to increase yields and encourage healthy plant development must use pruning and training strategies. Growers may maximize light exposure, airflow, and bud development by selectively removing leaves, regulating plant size, and employing various training methods. Remember to be cautious, to evaluate plant reaction, and to alter tactics as needed. You may increase yields and produce healthy, vigorous outdoor cannabis plants by using correct pruning and training strategies.

A cannabis plant requires a lot of nutrients, which it gets from the soil. A weed plant will grow OK on its own with decent soil, lots of sunshine and water, and a temperate atmosphere, but nutrients will assist the plant thrive and develop robust and strong.

What Are Cannabis Nutrients?

Growing high-quality weed necessitates the use of more nutrients, or fertilizer, than most other crops.

When transplanting a pot plant outside, outdoor cannabis farmers generally add powdered fertilizers to the soil. This will provide the plant with all or most of the nutrients it requires during its life cycle, and if you want to add extra nutrients later, you may do so by adding them to the surface of the soil, which is known as "top dressing."

Indoor gardeners usually use liquid fertilizers that they combine with water before watering their plants. Using liquid nutrients takes more time since you must measure and combine them in water 1-2 times each week.

We do not advocate putting indoor-growing fertilizers on outdoor plants since they are often constituted of synthetic mineral salts that can harm soil microbes.

What Nutrients Do Cannabis Plants Require?

Your marijuana plants require the following main nutrients, referred to together as macronutrients:

- Nitrogen (N)
- Phosphorus (P)
- Potassium (K)

These micronutrients are also required, although in much lesser amounts:

- Calcium (Ca)
- Magnesium (Ma)
- Sulfur (S)

Boron, chlorine, copper, iron, manganese, molybdenum, and zinc are some other micronutrients that exist in extremely minute levels and are less well-known.

Furthermore, cannabis plants obtain several non-mineral components from air and water:

- Carbon
- Hydrogen
- Oxygen

Cannabis plants require various levels of these nutrients at different phases of development: more nitrogen during vegetative growth, and more phosphorus and potassium during flower for bud production—also known as "bloom" nutrients.

Nitrogen

During the vegetative stage of a cannabis plant's life, nitrogen is primarily responsible for its development. It is a vital component of chlorophyll; without it, a plant cannot convert sunlight into energy and cannot develop.

Nitrogen is also found in amino acids, which serve as the building blocks for proteins in plants. Your cannabis plants will be weak and feeble if they lack the vital proteins. Nitrogen is also a component of ATP, which helps plant cells to govern how much energy they utilize. Nitrogen is also required for the production of nucleic acid, which is a component of DNA or RNA, and without it, cells cannot grow and proliferate.

Phosphorus

Phosphorus is required for the growth of big, healthy buds. This element's main function is to help make nutrients available for the plant to absorb. These nutrients are utilized to help a plant establish its structure as it grows from its roots to its blossoms.

Marijuana plants will exhibit evidence of underdeveloped roots and may not even blossom if not given enough phosphorus. The first indicators of phosphorus shortage are purple veins in the leaves.

Potassium

Potassium performs a variety of functions, the majority of which aid to control the processes that keep a plant healthy and thriving. It is important in osmoregulation, which is the passive regulation of water and salt concentrations in plants. Potassium achieves this via directing the opening and shutting of the stomata, which are the holes in the leaves through which plants exchange CO_2, H_2O, and oxygen.

Potassium also stimulates the formation of ATP, which acts to store the energy created during photosynthesis by producing glucose. This glucose is subsequently utilized by the plant as energy as it grows. Without enough potassium, you'll find weak, energy-starved plants that seem scorched because they can't efficiently manage the exchange of CO_2, H_2O, and oxygen.

Calcium

Calcium is crucial for holding the structure of a plant's cell walls together. Without calcium, new growth will not form correctly, and the plant will not operate effectively. New growth will be inhibited, leaves will curl, and the plant will develop rusty patches.

Magnesium

Magnesium is the essential component in chlorophyll, and plants cannot make glucose through photosynthesis without it. Without magnesium, sunlight cannot be transformed into energy.

Magnesium then aids in the metabolization of glucose, making it accessible for the plant to thrive. Without enough magnesium, the leaves will yellow and discoloration will spread to the veins.

How to Apply and Combine Cannabis Nutrients

Nutrient solution bottles and fertilizer bags will list the percentages of the three essential nutrients in the form of N-P-K: nitrogen, phosphorous, and potassium. For example, a product labeled "10-4-4" will have 10% accessible nitrogen, 4% phosphorus, and 4% potassium by weight.

A typical rule of thumb is that a vegetative fertilizer should have a high nitrogen content, a low phosphorus content, and a moderate potassium content, such as 9-4-5. Taper down the nitrogen and concentrate on phosphorus and potassium as the plant enters flowering—aim for a ratio of 3-8-7, for example.

Products are also commonly classified as "grow" solutions, which are high in nitrogen and required for vegetative growth, and "bloom" solutions, which are high in phosphorus and required for flower formation. If you don't want to become bogged down in numbers, stick to these broad phrases. Make careful to give your plants just water in the last week or two before harvest to eliminate any nutrient accumulation in the buds—this is known as flushing.

Nutrients in Liquid Form

Liquid fertilizers are commonly used for indoor gardening, although they may also be utilized outdoors. Liquid nutrients are used to weed plants in soil, hydroponics, and other grow media, and may be delivered easily and efficiently via drip lines, misters, and hoses.

Because liquid nutrients are easily available to the roots of a cannabis plant, they are fast-acting, which means they might harm plants if fed excessively. To combine liquid nutrients into water, you'll need a separate water tank, such as a specialized rubbish bin. You'll also need to know how much water each of your plants need. Depending on the amount of water required, add the appropriate ratio of liquid nutrients per the bottle's instructions.

When utilizing liquid fertilizers for cannabis plants, it's critical to write down and monitor a watering schedule:

- How much water do you consume?
- How many and what kind of nutrients are used?
- How often do you water?

You don't want to use liquid nutrients every time you water; instead, alternate between two watering on and one off. It is determined by the intricacy of your soil as well as the health of your plants. A surplus of fertilizers will harm your plants.

Giving weed plants the right quantity of nutrients necessitates close monitoring. Many gardeners begin with a lower solution dose than advised and gradually increase it until the plants react ideally. Too little nutrients result in stunted development, while too many might result in nutritional burn and lockout.

Check The Ph Of Your Water.

When combining fertilizers, it's critical to have a pH meter and a pH test kit on hand to check the pH level of your water. Cannabis grows best on soil with a pH of 6 to 7, and in hydroponic media with a pH of 5.5 to 6.5. Allowing the pH to go outside of this range can result in nutrient lockout, which means your plants are unable to absorb the nutrients they require, so test your water often and ensure the nutrient mix you feed them is within the ideal range.

The Significance of Time and Frequency in the Application of Nutrients and Fertilizers

Weed plants require a steady supply of nutrients as they grow. Create a feeding schedule that specifies when to water plants with nutrients and the quantities of nutrients required at each watering. Nutrient lockout can occur if nutrients are added at every watering, which is why growers avoid doing so. It's also a good idea to water with plain water.

Fertilizers are often placed into soil before a seed germinates or when a tiny plant is moved into new soil when used for outdoor growth. Additional fertilizer can be applied to plants as needed.

Can Cannabis Seedlings Or Clones Be Fertilized?

We do not advocate fertilizing or supplementing seeds, clones, or seedlings with additional nutrients. In its early phases, a plant is quite sensitive, and merely water will suffice.

The Best Nutrients for a Marijuana Plant during Its Vegetative Stage

Different nutrients will be required by a cannabis plant at various phases of its life. Cannabis plants require greater nitrogen during the vegetative period. These are often nutrients with the word "Grow" in the label, which aid the plant in packing on stems, branches, and leaves.

In the N-P-K system of nutrient ratios, this is the first letter, "N."

The Best Nutrients for a Marijuana Plant throughout Its Blossoming Stage

During blooming, a cannabis plant directs its energy into the production of buds, or flowers, rather than stems, branches, and leaves. When a weed plant flowers, it requires more phosphate and potassium and less nitrogen. These are commonly referred to as "bloom" nutrients.

In the N-P-K system of nutrient ratios, phosphorus is "P" and potassium is "K."

Cannabis Fertilizers That Are Organic

Organic fertilizers are nutrients derived from natural sources such as animal and vegetable waste. Sediments such as glacial rock dust and gypsum also offer useful elements for the soil and plants. They are commonly used for outdoor cultivation and are generally in powder form.

Organic fertilizers and nutrients are more adaptable than liquid nutrition. They often include fewer readily soluble nutrients and more components that benefit soil organisms.

Most of these fertilizers are inexpensive and may be purchased at your local nursery and sprinkled into soil before potting outside. If everything is done correctly, you will only need to water your plants once during the growing period because all nutrients are in the soil.

We propose the following organic fertilizers:

- **Nitrogen:** Worm castings, blood meal, fish meal, bat guano
- **Phosphorus:** Bone meal, rock dust
- **Potassium:** Wood ash, kelp meal
- **Calcium and magnesium:** Dolomite lime

Commercial soil blends also exist that already contain the proper mix of these nutrients.

Benefits of organic fertilizers for cannabis plants

Organic fertilizers are great since they enrich the soil while also boosting the quality of your plants. Other advantages include:

- Plants are protected against overnutrition by the gradual release of nutrients.
- Organic fertilizers will increase the quality and diversity of life in soil over time.
- Improved airflow and water retention in soil
- Renewable and long-term
- Organics remain in the soil, reducing the possibility of nutrient run-off.

Growing organically, according to some producers, improves the taste profile of processed cannabis while also increasing production. The fertilizing procedure may be repeated year after year as the soil improves—your soil will be even better next year than it was this year.

Organics are also beneficial if you wish to be more in tune with your natural surroundings. Organic fertilizers are easily obtained from renewable sources and are an environmentally beneficial solution.

Organic nutrient disadvantages for cannabis plants

Working with organic fertilizers has certain challenges. The biggest concern is that if your weed plants are nutrient deficient, it takes longer for a plant to absorb organic powder nutrients, which might exacerbate plant damage. Liquid nutrients work considerably faster. Other drawbacks include:

- They take time for the plant to absorb.

- Microorganisms are required to break down nutrients, which may take longer at colder temperatures.
- Insects and pests may be introduced.

What Is The Finest Soil For Cannabis Cultivation?

Cannabis plants prefer loamy soil that is neither too packed nor too loose. Some excellent brands are:

- PRO-MIX
- Fox Farms
- Happy Frog

Any of these businesses' standard potting soil will work well for weed plants. Mycorrhizae, a helpful fungus, will greatly benefit a plant's roots.

The cannabis blooming stage occurs when your plant transitions from vegetative development to bud production. It is triggered outside when daylight hours fall, and it is induced indoors by switching to a 12/12 light cycle. This is an important stage since the buds are the component of the plant that contains cannabinoids like THC.

Without a successful flowering period, your plant may not yield much, or what it does give may be of poor quality, thus additional care must be taken of your plants at this time.

How Long Does The Cannabis Flowering Stage Last?

Flowering lasts 8-12 weeks, however autoflower strains might be as brief as 6 weeks. This depends on the strain, with sativa dominated strains typically taking the longest. The end of the blooming stage is determined by trichome maturity, with most growers harvesting at the height of potency.

What Are The 5 Keys To A Profitable Flowering Phase?

- **Reduce Stress:** Keep the atmosphere steady. Changes in light, temperature, or humidity may all stress plants and impede bud growth.
- **Nutrient Optimization:** Change to bloom fertilizers that are high in phosphorus and potassium. Excess nitrogen might inhibit bud development.

- **Track Temperature and Humidity:** The ideal temperature range is 65-80°F (18-26°C). Humidity should gradually fall from 40-70% at the start of flowering to 40-50% at the conclusion.
- **Examine for Pests and Disease:** Inspect plants on a regular basis. To avoid further spread, remove any damaged areas as soon as possible. If necessary, use organic pest treatment.
- **Harvest at the Right Time:** If you harvest too early, the buds will be less powerful. If you wait too long, THC may begin to deteriorate. For the greatest results, wait until the majority of the trichomes are milky and the pistils are dark.

Stage of Pre-Flowering and First Signs of Flowering

When looking for early signs of blossoming in your plants, there are several elements to examine. This isn't really applicable if you're producing autoflowers because autoflowering kinds are pre-programmed to begin the flowering stage independent of external influences.

Photoperiod plants, on the other hand, begin to bloom one or two weeks after the lights are switched to 12/12. The earliest preflowers will resemble small white whiskers known as pistils; this is the first evidence of bud development.

Outdoor First Signs of Flowering

Growing outdoors completely relies on Mother Nature to perform all of the work. With no control over the light cycle, your cannabis plants will only begin to generate preflowers if daylight is reduced to less than thirteen hours. This is why, if you are growing outside, it is critical to arrange your grows around the weather in your area. You should try to time it so that your plants are ready to harvest before winter approaches. This usually involves harvesting your weed between September and November in the Northern Hemisphere.

The first indications of the flowering stage to watch for will be the same whether growing indoors or outdoors; it is just the time at which they begin to show that differs. Keep a look out for those pistils we discussed before, and you'll know the flowering period has begun.

How Do Buds Appear When They First Form?

Early bud growth begins with those little white pistils and progresses to something resembling a cannabis flower. You will observe the growth of some little green bobbles around the nodes where the pistils are developing from. These are called bracts and are the earliest indicators of the true bud.

It is critical to distinguish between the early symptoms of a female bloom and a male pollen bag. Pollen sacks emerge from the same location, but on male plants. If a male plant grows among your crop, the pollen sacks may explode, fertilizing the female plants and destroying your crop.

WEEK 1 OF THE FLOWERING STAGE (THE FLIP)

Cannabis plants grow rapidly during the vegetative stage and develop their distinctive structure, notably their foliage (leaves). Depending on the circumstances, they enter the pre-flowering stage, where development slows down, until they 'know' it is time to move to the blooming phase.

During the lengthy hours of daylight, a hormone called phytochrome (PR), which is created as soon as seeds germinate, is 'suppressed' by the red spectrum of light found in both the sun and artificial lighting. When plants experience at least 11 hours of unbroken darkness (some sativa kinds may require 12 hours or more), essential levels of PR are activated, and plants receive the signal to enter the blooming stage after around 5 days. Many growers refer to this technique as "the flip." When you flick the switch, the plant goes into panic mode and starts growing while also generating bud. Many strains will begin to develop fast for a few weeks before completely shifting into the blooming stage at this time.

Apart than that, there aren't many visible changes throughout the first week of blossoming. This is also an excellent time to examine particular training tactics, as cannabis requires time to recover from stress, and the blooming period should be focused on development rather than recuperation from stress or damage. Low-stress training (LST) approaches are perfect for this since they inflict less harm while allowing maximum light penetration to bud sites while smoothing down the canopy.

WEEK 2 OF THE FLOWERING STAGE (FIRST FLOWERING SIGNS)

This is the stage at which blooming marijuana plants begin to physically exhibit their new life cycle phase; however there is still some time before any buds appear. Little white whiskers known as pistils begin to appear from the area where fan leaves protrude from the plant's main stem about the second week after flipping (or around week 4 in auto-flowers). These are known as bud sites, and they will be the location to look for budding buds. If your plant produces sacs instead of pistils, you have guys in your garden, and you should get rid of them as soon as possible to avoid growing seeds and maximum bloom output.

While the plant's energy is focused on bud creation at this stage, the remainder of the plant is still developing. In fact, by the conclusion of flowering, your plants will have more than doubled in size since the switch. If you choose to continue LST or sculpt your plant for optimum bud creation, now is an ideal time to focus on bud growth locations and expose them to as much light as possible. If you want to add extra nutrients to your garden, such as boosters, now is the time to do it; just don't overdo it, since this might cause problems later on.

WEEK 3 OF THE FLOWERING STAGE (BUDS BEGIN TO FORM)

At this point, your cannabis plants will not have stopped growing entirely, and they might be up to 50% larger than they were when you turned off the lights. In week three of blooming, new stems and leaves emerge, and additional pistils may be seen sprouting from the leaf bunches above the main colas. Plants are still stretching and are fairly flexible at this point, so if you haven't done any sculpting yet, now is a good time to concentrate on that flat canopy, which may enhance your yields by up to 60% if you are growing a high yielding marijuana strain.

This is also the time to start paying attention to leaf tips and look for any nutrient imbalances (nute burn) that may be impeding your plants' growth. Plants will have enough time to recover from any possible nutritional deficiencies at this point, however the earlier you identify them, the simpler it will be for your plants to recover and produce a large crop.

As a general guideline, you should stick to a minimalist food plan to avoid nutritional imbalances (less is more). By the end of week 3, you should be able to see 'mini-buds' forming.

WEEK 4 OF THE FLOWERING STAGE (GROWTH HAS COMPLETED)

One month into blooming, vegetative development will have slowed to a halt, implying that plants will devote practically all of their energy to flower formation. Those small buds will become larger and thicker throughout the day, and some dazzling little trichomes will sprout on bud sites. However, increasing capitate trichomes result in higher odor, so if you don't have a plan for dealing with smells, now is a good time to create one. This is especially true for indoor stealth grows, where privacy and security are paramount issues.

Any extra bending or training will be unneeded at this point as the plants begin to take on their final shape for the home stretch. Depending on the cultivar in your indoor garden, you may need to use tactics like super-cropping to keep a flat canopy and pluck down any colas that have grown too near to the grow lights. This might be a concern, especially in grow rooms with limited space.

WEEK 5 OF THE FLOWERING STAGE (TRICHOMES BEGIN TO RIPEN)

At this point in the flowering cycle, your plants should have plainly identifiable buds with a considerable number of white pistils; however a few may have begun to turn a brownish orange. Trichome-covered buds will grow along the main cola as well.

Buds will begin to expand up and pack on some significant growth during the fifth week of flowering. Keep any that are particularly large since your plants may require some support at this time to avoid being burdened down.

At this stage, Trichomes should start to become cloudy/milky, which is also an indicator of increased terpene production, which means your garden will become a little stinky, so keep this in mind if odor is a concern. farmers should start thinking about lowering fertilizers and feeding in general around this time, as harvest is only a few weeks away and many farmers will prefer to flush their gardens for a week or two before harvest.

WEEK 6 OF THE FLOWERING STAGE (BEGIN INSPECTING YOUR TRICHOMES)

In week 6, buds continue to develop and slowly begin to mature, pistils begin to darken, and certain leaves, particularly fan leaves, begin to yellow and wilt. This is when everything starts to grow vibrant, much like your favorite fall forest. Many leaves will naturally defoliate (due to wilting, for example), but bigger fan leaves, particularly those at the plant's base, can be removed once discoloration is observed because the plant is now using other areas for photosynthesis.

Other leaves that aren't getting enough light, especially those at the plant's base, might be clipped to improve air circulation. This will also transfer the plants' efforts from delivering nutrients to the leaves to full-fledged bud formation. At week six, not all strains will be in the same development phase (some sativas take several weeks longer to completely mature), but the majority of indicas and many hybrids will have dense buds covered in sticky, pungent trichomes.

WEEK 7 OF THE FLOWERING STAGE (START FLUSHING YOUR CANNABIS PLANTS)

We're almost there, but there's still work to be done and things to keep an eye out for in order to reap that huge fat harvest. If you haven't cleansed your plants yet, now is the time; otherwise, the fertilizers you've been utilizing may have an impact on the ultimate result, particularly in terms of flavor. Simply halt routine feeding and give your plants some plain ol' water (distilled is probably ideal owing to its lack of mineral content) for the next several weeks before harvest to eliminate any mineral build-up and balance the pH of the soil.

Buds should develop rather thick by week 7, with swelling calyxes, orange-brownish pistils, and upright trichomes that now have some amber-colored caps filled with resin. These amber trichomes should account for around 10-15% of the mature trichomes visible on buds, with the remainder being generally cloudy/milky. When you've reached this level of maturity, you may begin counting down the days until the big chop.

If you want a balanced impact from your plant, 20-25% amber trichs is a good sign that your plants are about to ripen. Anything greater than 40-50% indicates that your flowers are overripe, and you may expect a severe couchlock-inducing effect. If you slice without a lot of amber trichomes, the impact will be more cerebral.

WEEK 8 OF THE FLOWERING STAGE: (PEAK RIPENESS AND HARVEST)

Peak ripeness occurs near the end of week 8. Plants are most vibrant at this point since the majority of the leaves should have turned red or yellow and the milky and/or amber trichomes should be fluorescing. If you're looking for the perfect time to photograph your grow, plants will be at their most beautiful around this time, so dust off your camera and click away.

THC levels are also at their maximum here, so if you want to keep as much as you can, don't wait too long and give your girls the chop. In addition to peak THC levels, your plants will be at their most pungent as female flowers urgently try to attract male pollen for seed formation, which we obviously want to prevent!

Cannabis types with an average blooming time of 8 weeks typically cease developing at this point and begin to degrade if not harvested. As previously stated, certain sativa-dominant types require many weeks longer than usual indica-dominant strains.

Trimming your cannabis flowers is an integral part of the cultivation process. Trimming your buds properly can improve their quality, potency, and total production. In this section, you'll learn all you need to know about trimming cannabis flowers.

Why Trim Cannabis Flowers?

Trimming cannabis flowers has several uses. First, it eliminates any extra foliage that may impede the growth of the buds. This helps the plant to direct its energy on generating high-quality blossoms rather than squandering it on leaves that will not contribute to the finished result.

Trimming enhances the overall look of the buds. Removing the leaves and other undesired materials results in a cleaner, more visually pleasing finished product. This is especially crucial for commercial growers who want to showcase their product in the best possible light.

Additionally, pruning can improve the potency of the buds. The buds have more trichomes, which are tiny glandular structures that create cannabinoids and terpenes, than the leaves. Removing superfluous leaves exposes more of the buds to light and air, allowing the trichomes to reach their maximum potential.

What Is Wet Trimming?

Wet trimming is the technique of clipping cannabis buds just after harvesting but before drying. Regardless of moisture condition, knowing how to trim cannabis is generally the same whether wet or dry.

Commercial farmers who trim wet are typically on a tight schedule and looking to expedite the post-harvest process. Wet trimming has several advantages, including mold avoidance, quicker drying, and the ability to place more buds on drying racks.

Trimming wet might also result in a much greater labor cost per pound. Growers who trim wet typically maintain harvesting crews on hand throughout the trimming operation. Commercial producers understand that it is unrealistic to maintain crews on hand while buds dry.

Trimmers are often paid by the weight. This means that a cannabis farmer is likely to pay a trimmer significantly more to work with a wet product than a dry one. When comparing wet versus dry pruning, most commercial companies find that the expenses exceed the advantages.

WHAT IS DRY TRIMMING?

Dry trimming is the technique of clipping dried cannabis buds before they are curing. The slower drying period helps to maintain the tastes and fragrances of the cannabis flower. This permits the compounds within the plant to mature at their ideal rate. This method also results in completed buds that are denser or more compact, making them more appealing for retail.

Keep in mind that a drier cannabis bud is more sensitive, and the brittle trichomes can be easily damaged if not handled with care. Because of the volume of plant material, the drying process takes up more area in a drying room.

Dry pruning might be more difficult if you've already sent your employees home while you wait for your hanging plants to dry. This has become essentially obsolete, with automated dry trimming equipment capable of processing up to 30 pounds per hour. Outpacing the quickest human trimmers, which may generate up to three pounds in an hour.

Essential Tools for Trimming Cannabis Plants

- **Pruning Shears:** High-quality pruning shears are essential for trimming cannabis plants, since they enable for accurate cuts without hurting the plant. To achieve the greatest results, choose shears with sharp blades and comfortable handles.
- **Gloves:** Trimming cannabis plants can be sticky job, so wearing gloves not only keeps your hands clean but also protects the buds from infection.

- **Trimming Tray:** A trimming tray with a built-in mesh screen may trap unwanted plant material and trichomes during the trimming process, making cleanup easier and letting you to save valuable kief for later use.
- **Scissors:** tiny, more precise scissors are perfect for trimming and removing tiny leaves from the buds. To maximize productivity, make sure the scissors are sharp and simple to clean.
- **Rubbing alcohol:** Rubbing alcohol is necessary for cleaning your trimming tools and keeping them sharp. Regular cleaning helps to avoid resin accumulation, which can result in inaccurate cuts and plant damage.

Trimming Procedures for Your Cannabis Plants

✓ Trimming the lower branches of the cannabis plant

Cannabis farmers commonly prune the bottom branches of their plants. This strategy redirects energy to the top of the plant, maximizing production. Because light provides better access to the bottom end of plants, the blooms are spread more uniformly among the branches, resulting in a more consistent output.

✓ Top your cannabis plants.

Topping is another popular training strategy among growers. It is suitable for both indoor and outdoor use, allowing you to successfully regulate the growth of your plants and appropriately manage the space in the growing area; it may also be useful if you want to keep a low profile outside. Topping is the process of removing your plant's growing tip, usually with a pair of clean, sterile scissors or a cutter, in order to avoid stress and insect symptoms.

When using this strategy, make sure to utilize common sense and respect the plant's development cycle. The optimal time to go is when it is fully developed but still has enough time to redirect energy to the target location, which is around 5 to 10 days before converting the photoperiod to 12/12 - right before the stretch. This ensures that the plant's structure has ample time to alter.

This training approach distributes plant auxins equally on secondary branches while also producing buds, resulting in increased growth and yield. Many growers also employ topping to care for their mother plants.

✓ Fimming your Cannabis plants

FIM stands for "fuck I missed" and is a technique that evolved from growers' blunders during topping. Similar to topping, fimming promotes bushy growth and enhanced lateral and upper branches.

This pruning technique involves cutting the head of tips rather than the full branch. You should trim around two-thirds of new branches so that the remaining portion regenerates and new heads grow, eventually turning into blooms. At worst, this will result in a new pair of shoots, and at most, five new pairs. And don't be concerned if the plant doesn't grow any new branches; this will merely transform your fimming into topping. As you can see, this procedure is absolutely safe and an excellent choice for mother plant care.

✓ Super cropping your cannabis plants.

Super cropping is becoming increasingly popular among cannabis farmers. It consists of softly breaking the inner fibers of the major branch terminals without totally cutting them. You must be very careful not to injure the outside tissue, since this may weaken the plant. A severe crack caused by excessive bending may result in the loss of the treated region, so use caution and patience. This strategy aims to limit the vertical growth of the top tips by forcing them to grow horizontally (once bent, they must be tied down) while increasing the vertical growth of the bottom branches. If done correctly, super cropping will result in consistent bud distribution and consequently much higher yields.

This approach may be used to increase yields and deal with challenging situations, such as limiting the development of a plant that is coming too near to the light and risking being burned.

Tips for Trimming Cannabis Plants

- **Patience and Precision:** Take your time cutting your cannabis plants. Rushing the process might lead to errors and have a detrimental impact on the end output. To achieve the greatest results, focus on making clean, accurate cuts.
- **Proper Lighting:** Adequate lighting is essential while pruning cannabis plants. Make sure your workstation is well-lit so you can correctly detect and remove undesirable leaves and stems.
- **Regular Cleaning:** To avoid resin accumulation and keep your trimming tools working properly, clean them with rubbing alcohol on a regular basis.
- **Comfortable Workspace:** Trimming may be a time-consuming operation, so make sure your workplace is comfortable and ergonomic to avoid strain and exhaustion.

- **Monitor the humidity and temperature:** When dry trimming, consider the humidity and temperature of your drying environment. Maintaining optimal conditions will assist to retain the strength and taste of your cannabis buds.

The final step in the cannabis production process is harvesting and curing the plant. Yes, there has been a lot of labor and management throughout the stages of growth, but now is when it all comes together.

Everyone adores the sort of smelly bud that, like the genie in Aladdin, escapes from a jar and fills the room! Growing with the greatest cannabis seed genetics - feminized, autoflower, or CBD - isn't enough to fully enjoy from such rich fragrances.

Cannabis buds will lose around 75% of their weight between harvesting and curing. With such a drastic shift in structure, adequate drying and curing is critical. As a result, the entire cannabis harvesting and curing process necessitates the correct combination of expertise, understanding, and patience.

Why Is The Cannabis Harvesting And Curing Stage So Important?

Terpenes, sometimes known as 'terps', are responsible for the distinct scents of various cannabis strains. There are about 200 terpenes in cannabis, with the most frequent being Limonene, Myrcene, Pinene, and Caryophyllene.

Weed that has been improperly cured will have lost these key odors and will frequently smell like hay or old lawnmower trimmings. There are several methods for improving the flavor of terpenes during the growth stages, but the focus of this chapter is on how to effectively enhance and keep the scent of weed during the harvesting and curing cannabis phases.

When Is The Optimum Season To Harvest Cannabis?

Harvesting cannabis at the pinnacle of perfection is a technique that novice producers must learn. Timing is critical in order to profit from the smelliest, tastiest harvest with the optimum intensity.

Here Are Few Keys:

- **Understand your strain:** Not all strains are made equal. It affects whether your plant is more indica or sativa, for example, and developing autoflowers has its own set of laws! The first rule of harvest is to adhere to the strain description parameters provided by the cannabis seed breeder.
- **Indications that buds are ready:** Buds will have grown much larger and the little hairs (pistils) that cover them will have changed color from white to red and brown. Buds have reached maturity when 50% of the pistils have changed from white to color.
- **The Trichome Test:** The most accurate signal is the Trichome Test, which states that buds are ready for plucking when the trichomes are 75% milky and 25% amber. The foregoing indicators imply that harvest time is approaching.
- **Selective harvesting:** Many farmers prefer to harvest everything at once, however this overlooks the plant's diverse ripening rates. The top buds are mature, but the bottom buds may require further time. Staggering bud harvesting takes longer (and costs more indoors), but it is typically worth the wait.

Finally, before you begin harvesting, don't forget to flush!

Weed Harvesting In the Open Air

The process of harvesting and curing cannabis is more difficult for outdoor farmers since there is little control over the weather and higher insect exposure in an outside setting.

As a result, the outside grower must consider a variety of issues. Nonetheless, there are some actions to perform before harvesting as well as instructions for harvesting outdoor weed.

Typical Cannabis Harvesting Issues and Solutions

Here is a list of some of the most frequent cannabis harvesting issues, along with some advice on how to avoid them.

- **Harvesting too soon.** As the blooming period comes to an end, it's easy to be misled by the sight of trichome-covered buds flashing beneath the grow lights and think they're ready. However, premature harvesting causes completed buds to lose strength, taste, and scent.

  Solution: Follow the harvest recommendations provided by the strain breeder and use the tried-and-true trichome test.

- **Trim work was poor.** It's a classic rookie error not to correctly clip buds before drying. Huge buds produced on huge stems and adding a coating of sugar leaf (because "it looked so crystally") are common mistakes.

  Solution: Do an excellent job at the beginning. Follow the trimming guide, which explains the wet and dry trimming methods.

Drying Cannabis for better Results

Drying is an important phase in the cannabis harvesting and curing process. It is critical to dry your cannabis buds properly in order to keep their beneficial properties and guarantee that the ultimate user experience is tasty, smooth, and pleasurable.

Factors That Contribute To Perfect Cannabis Drying Environment:

- **Create the dry space:** Cannabis buds require a cold, dark room or a separate drying facility with excellent ventilation to begin the drying process.

- **Is it hanging well:** Drying nets or lines are the most common means to hang freshly picked branches/buds to dry. Prepare them ahead of time and consider space constraints before deciding whether to utilize the 'wet' or 'dry' trim strategy.

- **Temperature and humidity control:** These are critical for a good drying operation. A temperature of 60-70°F (15-21°C) and a relative humidity of 45-55% are ideal.

- **Good air circulation:** Is vital for preventing mold formation while drying. Maintain a slight breeze using fans, but prevent direct airflow over the buds, which might cause them to dry out too rapidly. Take your time and don't attempt to rush the procedure!

- **Make sure the spacing is correct:** Giving the buds enough space to air and dry uniformly is critical whether using a drying net or hanging them from lines (made of cotton or fishing wire). When the drying space is overcrowded, moisture accumulates and mold grows.

- **Delicate handling is required:** When arranging the buds for drying, use a delicate touch, give them little treatment, and resist the impulse to compress them to prevent breaking off trichomes.

Common cannabis drying issues and solutions

- **Buds that are drying.** This is a classic harvesting and curing cannabis mistake; the buds appear dry, but after a few days in a storage jar, they are sweating as the interior moisture seeps out.

  Solution: The stem snap test is a great indicator (if the bud is dry, the stem will neatly snap; if it isn't, it will just bend). In a warm location, a plain brown paper grocery bag also works wonderfully!

- **Moldy buds in glass jars.** Mold will be a concern for the majority of producers during the growth period. Mold can grow on buds that have not been properly dried before keeping.

  Solution: Make sure the bud is completely dry before storing it in jars.

- **Buds that are too dried.** Cannabis buds that have been over-dried lose the necessary moisture that produces fragrant, delicious buds. Buds that break easily and have a harsh flavor are symptoms of over-drying.

  Solution: This problem may be resolved in storage jars. Adding little bits of orange peel or moist cotton balls, as well as employing humidity packs, are popular ideas.

- **Inconsistent drying.** This is common when all of the buds are combined together. Smaller buds dry faster, whereas bigger buds take longer.

  Solution: combine buds into comparable sizes throughout the drying process and preserve them together in storage jars during the curing phase.

Curing cannabis for optimal results

The final harvesting and curing cannabis step will determine the quality of your finished product. The curing process is an art form. So, how can you know whether you're on the correct track? Well, it's frequently simpler to tell when you're incorrect! When you open that storage jar and the aroma is a little'meh,' you know you still have some work to do.

Another common error that far too many growers do is to hasten this procedure. Yes, you want to get in there and eat the fruits of your labor! But it's always worth the wait to get the full gratifying experience of eating properly cured cannabis buds.

How Long Should Cannabis Be Cured?

Every grower will have their own opinion on this aspect of the cannabis harvesting and curing procedure. In general, the curing duration can range from two to eight weeks, while most producers advocate curing marijuana for three to four weeks to obtain the best scent.

Why Is Cannabis Treatment Important?

Cannabis buds that have been freshly plucked have a 'green' tinge to them. The smell and taste are abrasive, and they are frequently associated with a 'hay'-like character. The effect might alternatively be more 'racy'.

This is due to the fact that the buds still retain different substances at this stage, including starch and, most importantly, chlorophyll. Curing therefore calms the buds, similar to letting wine 'breathe' or a baked cake 'rest' to enhance strength, fragrance, and flavor.

Curing, burping, and preserving marijuana buds

A home grower must take a number of critical measures during this stage of the cannabis harvesting and curing process.

Choose the correct curing container: A glass preserve jar, which is often used for jam making and preserving fruits and vegetables, is the finest container to utilize. They contain a rubber seal to guarantee that the contents are vacuum packed tightly, preventing air from getting in or out.

Fill the jar to the desired level: Not too tight, to enhance airflow circulation, fill the jar to 75% full.

Store it correctly: It must be kept in a cold, dark area. A fridge or a cool cupboard would suffice.

'Burping' buds method: This is the traditional method for removing moisture from the buds/jar:

- **First week:** Open the jar twice a day and keep it open for a few minutes each time. Excess moisture evaporates, lowering the likelihood of mold growing on buds.
- **Following weeks:** Gradually reduce the procedure from every day to every other day, and eventually every few days. You can notice the difference - the scent will get more fragrant as time passes.

Use a humidity pack: If utilizing the burping buds approach causes too much uncertainty, consider using items that manage moisture levels. A humidity pack is a simple approach to regulate moisture.

CONCLUSION

Finally, "The 21st Century Cannabis Farming" is an excellent resource for navigating the ever-changing terrain of cannabis growing in today's world. From the growth of regulatory frameworks to the new technology that shape the sector, this book gives a deep perspective of the possibilities and problems that cannabis producers face today.

As we recognize the plant's potential for medicinal, recreational, and industrial applications, it is critical to approach cannabis cultivation with a combination of scientific understanding, environmental management, and a dedication to responsible methods.

By being aware and adaptive, we can contribute to the cannabis industry's long-term success while also having a good influence on people and communities. May this book encourage a new generation of forward-thinking farmers who are committed to creating the future of cannabis growing in the twenty-first century.